SELF LOVE

A SIMPLE GUIDE TO BEING YOUR TRUE SELF

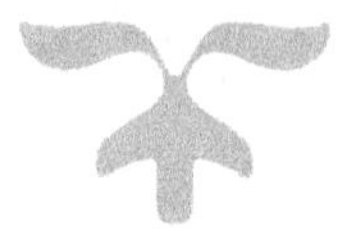

SEPTEMBER 10, 2022

ROXANNE HILL

HILL PUBLISHERS

Cover design by: HILL

Library of Congress Control Number

Printed in the United States of America

DEDICATION

THIS WORK IS DEDICATED TO MY BEING ABLE TO FIND MY TRUE SELF AND LOVE ME FOR BEING ME.

TABLE OF CONTENTS

INTRODUCTION

SELF LOVE IS A BOOK WRITTEN WITH HOPES THAT EVERYONE WILL FIND HAPPINES WITHIN US AND SEE THE VALUE AND POTENTIAL WE ALL POSSESS

PREFACE

Until you are capable of forgiving yourself and others, you cannot grow and thrive. Keep in mind that extending forgiveness is a selfish act. You show them forgiveness so that you will have the energy to focus on your own growth. Take ownership of your mistakes. Nobody is perfect. Being overly critical of yourself or others won't make you more successful.

CHAPTER ONE
GETTING STARTED WITH SELF-LOVE
SINCERE LOVE

When the topic of self-love is brought up, far too many people turn up their noses, as if it were a little cheesy and self-indulgent. However, one of the most significant and effective things you can accomplish in life is to learn to love yourself. Your heart is your source of strength, and everything changes when you turn it into the source of love in your own life. When you begin to love yourself, everything in your life improves—your relationships, your work, and even your health.

But even while we all know in our hearts that it's crucial to love oneself, we find that the challenge most individuals have is figuring out how to accomplish it.

We like to consider self-love as a skill that can be developed over time via practice. When we practice self-love, we create a loving and healthy relationship with ourselves, and something miraculous happens — we become our own best friends.

To love oneself is the start of a lifetime relationship, as Oscar Wilde once stated.

So how do we start that romance? How do we develop self-love?

Here are seven ways to immediately begin practicing the art of self-love:

Feed yourself with love,

If you've never practiced self-love before, start by putting your attention on taking care of yourself. The most fundamental manifestation of self-love is feeding oneself, so this week, pay attention to what you put in your body and give it what it needs. Start your day with a green smoothie, reward yourself with a raw chocolate snack, and schedule some time to prepare a healthy supper packed with superfoods for yourself. Our eating habits are a reflection of how much we value ourselves. Therefore, if you practice self-nourishment, you'll build a solid foundation for self-love.

Take yourself on a date.

Make this the first time you've ever gone on a date with yourself. Spending a lot of time and care on our bodies allows us to express our personalities and want to love ourselves. Our physical well-being has a direct impact on how we feel about ourselves. We frequently experience loneliness and a lack of affection because we are disconnected from our bodies. You want to maintain the vigor and energy in that wonderful physique of yours. Therefore, you must include activities that make you feel fantastic in your body in your self-love regimen, whether they be yoga, running, 80s Aerobics, or dancing like Beyonce (a particular favorite of ours)!

Display personality

Finding authentic methods to express yourself and allowing yourself to be wholly you is crucial. Everyone has a passion, whether it be for pottery, poetry, dancing, writing, singing, acting, sculpting, cooking, DJing, or any other creative endeavor. In many cases, it was something we did naturally as kids. We always experience something to make us feel completely alive.

And what about you? When do you think you'll be able to completely let go and be yourself? Consider your past behavior if you don't currently engage in it. What energizes you and allows you to connect with your innermost self truly? Now go create space in your schedule for it. It's crucial that you make time for the activities that allow you to truly express yourself from the heart, whether it's dancing like Rihanna, singing like no one is listening, or painting in big bold strokes just for joy.

Compose a love letter to yourself.

Pick up a pen, and write a letter to yourself with the same love and affection you would for a close friend. Write about the events and persons in your life that make you happy at the moment and that inspire, motivate, and show kindness to you. Consider how you're feeling, give yourself a pep talk if necessary, and write down your goals and aspirations for the future. If there is something in your life that you are currently battling with, see what guidance and inspiration you can offer to yourself. Then, be sure to acknowledge your successes and end your letter with love. After that, post the letter and look forward to getting it a few days later.

Fill yourself with good vibes.

No matter where we are or what is going on in the world, we have much more ability than we frequently realize to create the sentiments we want to feel in life. All we need to do is learn how to access those emotions. Finding a photo of yourself that makes you feel that way just by looking at it is a simple method to do this. Think of a period in your life when you were full of pleasure, happiness, peace, or fulfillment - whatever it is you want to feel - and then find that photo.

Make the picture your phone's screensaver or print it out and hang it on your bathroom mirror so you can view it every day. Take a peek at that image whenever you need a pick-me-up and allow yourself to soak up those positive emotions.

BEING TAUGHT TO LOVE ONESELF

One of my greatest achievements is discovering how to love oneself. I say that because of how long I fought this struggle without giving up, how much energy I invested in the battle, and

because loving who you are is the greatest gift and the most beautiful thing there is.
Since I was aware of my differences from my peers throughout my childhood and well into adulthood and had to battle this perception of difference in order to move toward self-love, I view my efforts to develop self-esteem as a struggle.
Right now, I feel like nobody or nothing can break my spirit or make me into someone I'm not. I gained a lot of inner strength and self-love from the realities that follow:

You stand out and are special.
No one in the entire world is exactly like you. Don't try to be someone else; this is how it should be. If not, the world is not getting the genuine you!

You are not alone in this
Why isolate yourself by believing that you are the only one who is struggling when obstacles and emotional baggage are something that everyone deals with? When you're feeling low, it's easy to slip into this trap, but you owe it to yourself to resist this temptation.

Embrace who you are.
At all costs, make an effort to accept or, even better, embrace who you are. If not, you are committing yourself to a lifetime of misery. I find it helpful to conceive about autism, or whatever issue you are facing, as a "profile" or as a distinctive feature of

your identity. Being able to think in these terms can help you arrive at self-acceptance.

Decide who you are and be that person.

You need to clarify what you believe in, what is essential to you, and what you stand for. Don't let others act on your behalf. Being kind to yourself and others, standing up for your own wants and interests (doing so is not a selfish act), and devoting time to activities you are good at and like doing will all contribute to developing inner strength.

Avert thinking "myself vs them"

I've learnt to think in terms of "We are all human" rather than "there's me, and then there's everybody else" or "I am not neurotypical like they are." Celebrate your uniqueness, embrace your "neurodiversity," and remember that despite our differences, everyone and everywhere is still a human being.

Learn about and develop your skills, interests, and capabilities.

I started enhancing my sense of self at a young age by devoting time to honing my skills and enthusiasm in a variety of interests. Over time, music would develop into a fundamental part of who I am rather than just one of my talents. My Aspie profile has also given me skills that have been very useful to me. For instance, I am especially analytical, half-empty, and detail-oriented, just like many people on the autistic spectrum. and skilled at "outside the box" thinking.

Keep in mind that a glass of water that is half full will never be empty.

Don't give up if you become diverted when working toward a goal. Consider mistakes and hardship as teaching opportunities that can help you develop and become stronger rather than letting them bring you down and keep you down.

Get assistance and guidance.

Take help if you need it if you're having problems. Furthermore, don't dismiss yourself as a helpless person just because you require assistance. Possibly, we might all benefit from a little assistance once in a while.

Your interpersonal interactions have an impact on how you feel about yourself.

My inner sense of self was undermined throughout those years since I frequently behaved and spoke without care for others when I was younger, more introverted, and less conscious. There is a direct correlation between how you treat people and how you see yourself. Make use of this truth to your benefit.

Be conscious of the personalities of the individuals you associate with.

I've learned over the years to seek out intelligent, content, and successful people; to pursue friendships with people who could see the good in me despite my shortcomings in social skills. Focus on developing connections with nice, receptive, and intriguing people.

Self-love requires reasonable expectations.

Everybody experiences hardship and unfairness in life. Other people have their own issues to handle, therefore they won't always be able to fulfill my expectations of them. I was able to better understand other people and take into account their circumstances when I started to put myself in their situations. As a result, I developed more self-confidence and became less reliant on other people to make me happy. I also learned how to modify the expectations I had for both them and for myself.

A virtue is patience.

My entire life has been consumed with my "inner war for self-love." Remember that nothing comes together overnight if, like me, you have been traveling down a winding road for a while and are still not where you want to be. Accept mistakes, be kind to yourself, and keep moving forward!

Meaningful change requires numerous tiny actions made over a long period of time, is challenging, slow to occur, and frequently accomplished in the face of adversity. Change needs these components in order to be effective and long-lasting. Do you feel up to the task? I hope you are. You merit it.

Sam Farmer is a self-advocate for the neurodiverse community, a writer and author, a public speaker, and a consultant for Flores, a busincss that uses virtual reality technology to teach social, communication, and other life skills to neurodiverse people. A person who received an autism diagnosis later in life produces blogs and articles, creates coaching videos and podcasts, and gives presentations at conferences and support groups, sharing tales and ideas about how to be happier and more successful in the face of difficulty and hardship.

PERSONAL DEVELOPMENT

How To Actually Love Yourself: A 6-Step Process

It's so easy to describe “Loving yourself" and difficult to describe how to do it. Learn how to gradually start loving yourself more each day by putting these six steps into practice:

Step 1: Accept responsibility for your feelings and be open to experience discomfort.

Following your breath consciously is the first step towards becoming present in your body and accepting all of your emotions. It's about turning toward your emotions rather than pushing them away through various sorts of self-abandonment, such as being mentally sharp, critiquing yourself, abusing substances to dull the pain, etc. Every emotion contains information.

Step 2: Enter the learning mindset.

Make a commitment to learning about your emotions, including any that may be hurting you, so that you can move toward acting lovingly.

Step 3: Learning false beliefs.

Step 3 is a thorough and kind process of exploration that involves learning about your beliefs and conduct as well as what is going on with a person or circumstance that might be the source of your sorrow. Ask yourself, your inner child: "What am I doing or thinking that causes the painful feelings of anxiety, depression, guilt, shame, jealousy, anger, loneliness, or emptiness?" Allow the answer to come from inside you.
Ask your ego about the concerns and false beliefs that are motivating the self-abandoning thoughts and behaviors after you have identified what you are thinking or doing that is producing these sensations.

Step 4: Start a conversation with your higher self.
Connecting with your higher guidance is simpler than you might imagine. Being willing to learn how to love oneself is the key. The solutions might appear right away or gradually. They might appear to you in words, pictures, or dreams. The solutions will appear once your heart is willing to learn.

Step five: Take Actions of love
Sometimes individuals believe that "loving oneself" is a state of mind. Instead, then focusing on how to feel love for yourself, a helpful method to approach loving yourself is by emphasizing the action: "What can I do to love myself?"

By this time, you've already begun to talk about your feelings, progressed into learning, acknowledged your grief, and accessed your spiritual direction. One of the loving actions you mentioned in Step 4 must be performed in Step 5. Even though they may start out small, these actions add up over time.

Step 6: Review what you did and start over if necessary. Check in after you have taken the loving action to see if your anger, pain, and humiliation are being healed. If not, you repeat the process until you find the truth and take the kind of loving actions that give you peace, joy, and a strong sense of your own intrinsic worth.

You will eventually come to realize that loving yourself enhances every aspect of your life, including your relationships, physical and mental health, capacity for manifesting your dreams, and self-esteem. The secret to being able to love and connect with others and build loving relationships is to first love and connect with yourself. The secret to living a passionate, contented, and joyful life is to love yourself.

Reset Your Gut

34 Ways to Love Yourself and Take Care of Yourself

You can achieve a higher level of safety and happiness by loving yourself.

Since it is how we discovered security and love as children, we tend to go outside of ourselves for love. For our good deeds, we received rewards. The truth is that you can only find the love you seek within.

But despite this, we continued to hunt for affection in other people. Because of this, no amount of love from another person will satisfy you completely, and if you don't have faith in your abilities, you'll never feel safe.

But how can you fall in love and gain confidence?

To overcome our limiting beliefs and live a life that truly shines, we focus on loving ourselves.

Love for oneself is the key to solving all problems. You could be kind to yourself and, as a result, improve as a person by engaging in self-love.

How to Learn to Love Yourself

Give yourself a well worth break. Take a few deep breaths, give yourself a little embrace, and start teaching yourself how to love yourself.

1. Throw out the notion that you must be flawless.

Start by giving up the idea of being flawless in every manner, including your physique, life, and IQ, if you're wondering how to practice self-love. The ideal of perfection is unattainable, and it usually masks major mental health issues when you see it on social media.

Never aim for perfection. Knowing that nobody is is a good thing. Everyone has their own unique qualities and personalities; nobody aspires to an idealized level of perfection.

2. Recognize that societal expectations can often present unrealistic methods.

You cannot legitimately the same with others, since you are unique on this planet. The only person you should compare yourself to is yourself.

Comparison is the thief of joy, according to Theodore Roosevelt.

Even if you achieve that unachievable level, your hunger for more will never go away since it is ingrained in human nature to constantly be insatiably curious. You'll feel horrible about yourself and miserable if you compare yourself to that unrealistic ideal. Keep in mind that we lose ourselves more when we compare.

3. Every day, try to live in the present for just a moment. Look within you to get the best in life. Acknowledge the past with the miracle in the today. Recognize your gratitude for being a live, breathing, and active human being.

According to Psychology Today, mindful individuals frequently exhibit higher levels of self-worth, greater empathy, and greater security.

4. Everyday Gratitude
The secret to happiness and self-love is daily thankfulness.

Take three minutes each day to reflect on all the things for which you are grateful, such as your health, your life, your friends, your country, M&Ms, how long that old pan has lasted you, or how the person on the bus let you off first. You can start a gratitude journal, an Instagram account, a blog, or just do this.

We become resentful when we become comfortable. Change that and express thankfulness daily. Gratitude, according to Harvard Health, can increase your feelings of happiness and, as evidenced by research, can enhance your general welfare.

5. Accept That There Are Some Things You Can't Control
You can only change the things you can change, which includes your reactions. Have awareness that you can't change the people around you, influence them or change their way of thinking.

Don't try to control everything in life; instead, concentrate on how you react to it. Instead of trying to control everyone and everything, do the best you can and then put your hands up and declare, "It is in the hands of the Gods now." Gods will be done.

6. Self-Care
Taking care of ourselves is seen as selfish by society, and, God forbid, this is what we fear the most. In response, we work really hard to demonstrate our goodness to everyone.

Putting yourself as the top priority should always come first and nothing should change that. Happiness = Self-Love + Self-Care.

7. Check Your Emotional Well-Being
Take a seat, order a coffee, and talk about your day's activities. How are you feeling? Feel that emotions. Learning to feel your emotions rather than suppressing them is the best course of action. If you want to continue practicing self-love, staying in touch with your emotions is vital.

This includes unfavorable ideas. Are they real? Do they show any benefit? Are they moral?

Think about if anything you're about to say will help you before you say it. Does having this thought make me better in any way? Or is it just rude, dismissive, and severe?
One of the most important steps to pleasure is to stop internal suffering since we frequently mistreat our brains. Preach words of encouragement to yourself and believe them. Self-love will always be hampered by negative thoughts.

8. Constrict Your Circle
Your entire existence is impacted by your social network.

Look at the five people you spend the most time with because they shape who you are. Are they true? Loving? Supportive? Or are they rude, offensive, and unfavorable? Do they regard themselves highly?

Remember that you owe no one anything, especially if they are pulling you down. Examples include a pessimistic buddy, an insulting partner, or an overbearing aunt with strong opinions. They owe you nothing in terms of your time. Discard, stay away, and carry on.

9. Eat well.
What you ingest has an impact on your mental wellness. You sit and feel ashamed of yourself if you consume something you

consider to be awful, not just physically but also psychologically.

Make yourself proud live a little and don’t wallow in past mistakes. Living life to the fullest Eat healthy foods that you like to show yourself love. It will be appreciated by your body.

10. Get to it!

Don't just sign up for a gym and never go. Find a sport or physical activity that you enjoy, that makes you giggle, after trying out a new one. Do that now!

There are essentially an endless number of various sports, including dancer, spin, mermaid swimming, and Zumba. Try them out and watch your happiness grow! Even if you have a busy schedule, there are various ways to stay active. Here is a workout video that you can complete in 7 minutes.

11. Make Your Environment Cleaner

Get rid of everyone who is negative on social media. All those funny memes about ineffective drunks. Simply put, it makes sense to surround yourself with good knowledge because doing so will help you live a happier life since you are the product of your thoughts.

12. Be Special

If you want to learn to accept yourself, embrace your uniqueness and learn to love who you are as a person. This is what sets you apart. Loving yourself should be the word of the days.

13. Eliminate Negative Relationships

Cut off all unhealthy connections. Seriously. If somebody in your life makes you feel anything less than great, they shouldn't be there. It could take some effort to identify the relationships in your life that are harmful.

It's important to think about the relationships that make you feel good and to identify those that have a negative impact on your life. You should not surround yourself with those that don't support you.

14. Accept Yourself

Do you remember the one or more occasions you did anything that made you feel bad about yourself, embarrassed, or ashamed? Leaving the past and focusing on the future. Even while you can't undo what you've already done, you can have an impact on what occurs in the future.

Think at it as a learning opportunity and have faith in your ability to improve. Be kind to yourself as you would be kind to someone else if they were flawed.

15. Meditate

Every day, set aside some time to relax your head. Inhale and exhale, clear your mind of all thoughts, and then just be. To be more deliberate, try meditation.

Be aware of your desires, feelings, and thoughts. Live a life that accurately show your improvements. By implementing mindfulness techniques into your routine, you can incorporate self-reflection.

16. Always remember who you are

You have faced many challenges, yet you have overcome them all, becoming stronger with each one. Do not forget who you are, please.

Adversity should be welcomed since it will enrich your life and enable you to achieve your goals. It's normal to feel self-doubt, but try not to let it dominate your thoughts.

17. Give Your Body the Love It Deserves

Your body is a beautiful and wonderful tool for discovery. Your body wasn't designed solely with the rest of the world's aesthetics in mind. It’s not an obligatory something. You can use it as a tool to achieve all of your life's objectives.

As if it were your child, take good care of your body as you climb, eat, travel, commute to work, and knit. Only love, and the understanding that everything is perfect just the way it is. Self-love is all about adoring your appearance and loving yourself unconditionally!

We're told having the perfect figure will make us happy. You are likely familiar with that kind; it is a commonly airbrushed-over unrealistic beauty standard.

Regardless of how much you diet, how many things you buy, or how much plastic surgery you get. Happiness has no home in the body; thus, it cannot exist there.

Accepting oneself is the first step to happiness. Recognize that you need a body to feel successful, in control, and able to achieve everything you desire.

Stop wasting time trying to adhere to a specific diet type and instead focus on finding Happiness since you can do whatever you want no matter how your body is shaped. It is discovered within.

18. Attempt minimalism

Enjoying your belongings and experiences, not your goods, is the only way to find true joy and love.

You want someone to congratulate you on your excellent life and for completing all of your goals when you pass away! Not that you were a hoarder or amassed a lot of stuff. Being content with what you already have can lead to amazing discoveries like creating a nutritious supper from scratch.

19. Make a list of your strengths.

The next time you feel happy and in charge of the world, make a list of your best qualities and accomplishments. Even while it may seem corny, it might serve as a helpful reminder when you are having a bad day. Doing this gives you a solid source of strength, despite the fact that it might be difficult at first.

20. Never be afraid to be original.

To express yourself, use your creativity and whatever other tools you see fit. Leave your inner critic at the door and focus on whatever captures your attention—painting, writing, sculpting, building, or music. When it comes to creativity, there are no rules.

According to Forbes, creativity can actually be good for your health.

21. Learn Always

Try new things, read, and learn new things. Discover what functions best for you.

Try. Please read this as well. Well, that's interesting, you think, and you walk away. Decide which one to use, then put it into action. Being happy is a daily practice, not a switch.

22. Don't be too hard on yourself

Don't believe everything you see. Everybody has a critic who wants to keep them small and safe. The negative aspect is that it keeps us from living full lives. Being harsh on oneself is one of the main things that could keep someone from liking oneself.

23. Reduce Stress

Work on a favorite stress-reduction strategy for 10 minutes. Managing illnesses including potential heart disease, obesity, high blood pressure, and depression can be facilitated by stress prevention.

24. Placing Time-Boundaries

If you ask yourself "how to love yourself," the answer is to start by putting yourself first. Establish limits for how you will use your time. Avoid time-consuming activities that don't enhance your life.

Additionally, don't feel bad about saying no. Saying no periodically does not make you a bad person; rather, it makes you more realistic

25. Leaving your comfort Zone

Taking a risk is a good way to show yourself, love. The happiness we feel when we realize we have achieved something we didn't think was possible is wonderful.

26. Love and respect one another

When we treat others like we want to be treated, we feel better about ourselves. Even if someone doesn't always reciprocate the favor, it's their problem, not yours.

27. Commemorate achievements

Whether they are large or small, celebrate your accomplishments. Compliment yourself on all little achievement is a step to loving yourself

28. Adhere to Your Passion

Do you know what frightens and thrills you at the same time? The thing you want to do, even though you've convinced yourself it won't work. ACT FAST AND WISE!

Self-love is a changing idea. It can take a lifetime to master, but practice is the key. Be kind to yourself and keep going through the difficult times, especially if you're trying to discover your passion.

29. Give up the need for other people's approval

"You can be the ripest, juiciest peach in the world, and there's still going to be someone who hates peaches.

You can love yourself without needing other people's approval. Finding your happy place and healing from previous trauma and wounds can both be accomplished by letting go of your need for other people's approval. Our desire for acceptance can occasionally be linked to prior occurrences.

In actuality, it seems almost like a load has been lifted when we let go of the things that have happened to us. It's no longer necessary for us to transport that. Better is due to us.

30. Choose a happy location

What is the one thing you can think of that makes you feel fully at rest, at peace, joyful, upbeat, and full of life? When you're going through a challenging time, go there or see yourself there. Think about how something seems, feels, and smells. Make it a practice to think about your happy place frequently.

31. Turn off and move inside

Take a seat by yourself for a bit with a cup of your choice tea, coffee, wine, or other beverage. No TV or other distractions, just you. Think about the wonderful things that are currently happening in your life, your biggest goals, and the most effective means to achieve them.

32. Make a journal.

How do you feel when you have so many thoughts going through your head? List all of them on paper, regardless of how absurd, harsh, upsetting, or horrific they are.

Do whatever it takes to let it go for you. Keep a journal with it. Regular journaling can be a vital part of your self-love routine and will aid in your developing appreciation of its benefits.

33. Be practical

On our globe, happiness does not exist every second of the day. Do you comprehend the rationale? After all, we are all human. We all make mistakes and experience conflicting emotions, and that's okay. Acknowledge your humanity.

By exercising it, you can create a realistic mindset. Being realistic will help you on your journey to self-love because we are frequently too harsh on ourselves.

34. Laugh

Laughter has numerous positive effects and is a kind of self-care. Learn to laugh at yourself and have fun throughout the day.

Final Reflections

Learning to love yourself and practice self-love will help your relationship. If you want to build a solid relationship with other people, you must do this. You will surely get better at developing self-love, even though it takes time.

Despite your worry, take stock of everything you've already achieved. Once you learn how to be nice to yourself, you will be one step closer to becoming the finest version of yourself.

excellent experience Get moving and engage in the things that excite your interest. Take in your great life, enjoy who you are, and enjoy them.

Seven Incredible Things Occur When You Start Loving Yourself More

"Once I learned to love myself sufficiently, I started letting go of unhealthy things. This included other people, my profession, my personal views and routines—anything that made me feel small. In my opinion, that was disloyal. I now perceive it as self-love.
~Kim McMillen

I've been studying self-love for a very long time.
In fact, I started learning about self-love so long ago that I was quite irate when a Peruvian shaman informed me fifteen years later that it was the solution to all of my problems!

As a teen, I had experienced depression. I had a really depressing life for almost two years. To be honest, I barely remember anything. I experienced the suffering of life. I kept to myself. It seemed like there was a new challenge to face every day. I didn't live; I existed. I eventually conquered it and found some resources that I still use to help me through any low points I may experience now. One of them was learning to love oneself.

Every day, I wrote affirmations. I kept working on my mirror. I began to appreciate myself more and treat myself kindly. I routinely meditated, slowly rebuilding myself. I believed I had self-love down pat. I genuinely believed I knew what self-love meant.

I was mistaken.

I was unmarried and not too happy about it when I was in my early thirties. I'm not happy with my corporate career. Living in a converted garage in London and thinking what to change in my life to feel happier.

I had no second thoughts when my friend inquired if I would be interested in visiting Peru.

It appeared to be the ideal excursion at the ideal time.

Three weeks were fantastic for us. We traveled to several historic sites, took part in religious rituals, interacted with shamans, met them, and collaborated with them. We also stopped by some ancient settlements that were leading simple lives in the Andes. We took advantage of all Peru had to offer.

My friend and I made the decision to go for a coca leaf reading one day. As with prior readings, I was mostly curious, but I also wanted reassurance that my life was going to change and that I would soon be in a better place.

I now understand better than to seek the comfort of a psychic. A psychic once told me that depending on our choices, there are a few future possibilities for us. I thus began to have greater confidence in my decisions and to feel at ease with uncertainty because there is always a solution to our difficulties. I also have faith that everything I am going through is for my best interests and will teach me the lesson I need to learn right now.

Returning to my story, we entered a rear room of a very dilapidated massage parlor that we had discovered a few days previously.
The shaman arrived and established himself. Since he couldn't speak English, a Dutch translator was available.
My friend approached her first, asked her questions, and received advice.
When it was my turn, I began to ask the typical queries, such as When will I find the one? When will I discover a better position? What kind of employment is it? Will I ever find a nicer apartment? When can I expect to start making more money?
The shaman swirled the leaves in his hands and threw them up after I asked the first question. He remarked to me, "When you start loving yourself," after they had fallen.
Okay, I reasoned to myself as I posed a new query.
The shaman flung the leaves once more, gave me a moment to think, and then replied, "When you start loving yourself more."
Silently nodding in agreement with him, I said, "Okay." I still believed I had room to love myself more.
I questioned again and received the same response. I asked another question and received the same response.
I started to have some doubts and felt a little apprehensive.

Going to a shaman we didn't know and that no one had recommended to us made me feel like we were being a little foolish.
I snapped after I received the same response five times.

I yelled at the translator and accused the shaman of being a fake and incompetent.
The translator attempted to calm me down by assuring me that the shaman was well-liked and knowledgeable in his field. It seems like a lot of people kept going back to him because his readings were so accurate.
It was difficult to believe, somehow.
After finishing the reading, we departed.
My friend attempted to explain this incident to me, but I utterly discounted it.
I was enraged. Not even the reading, but rather the understanding that I had put so much effort into my work on self-love and believed I was capable of loving and respecting myself. However, a total stranger was here reminding me that I still had work to do.
How much effort on self-love do I need to do before I genuinely start loving myself? I can still remember asking my friend angrily. Is fifteen years not enough?"
I was discouraged and felt powerless.
I had the impression that the self-improvement work I had done up until that point in Peru had been in vain.

Because of all the introspective work I had done, I felt like I ought to have known better, which is why I was frustrated. I ought to have drawn better-looking men. I ought to have had a better position. I ought to have made more cash. I ought to have been more joyful.

Before I truly understood what self-love was, I still had some more lessons in life to learn.

A few years later, I was still unmarried despite numerous unsuccessful dates with men who didn't even faintly meet the description of my ideal man, and I was even more unhappy in my new work. Not much happier, I had a moment of realization when I was drying my hair.

I suddenly felt it hit me. I experienced what it was like to love oneself completely. I experienced a sudden outpouring of self-love. Kindness and compassion for myself swept over me.

I became aware of how unloving I was of myself at that time. I came to the conclusion that I had been betraying and forsaking myself my entire life.

I was able to fully comprehend what the Peruvian shaman truly meant.

I wouldn't be able to gain a better career, meet a loving man, or feel happier until I fully liked and valued myself.

I couldn't feel worthy of it all because I didn't love myself enough.

It took me some time to process these revelations and understand how my love—or lack of love—for myself was

directly responsible for my unfulfilling romantic relationships, draining profession, and general lack of satisfaction in life.
I now have my own notion of self-love after a few years.
For a very long time, I thought that self-love was just how I felt about myself.
Now that I am wiser, Much more than just a feeling, it is.

Self-love is a practice for me. It involves choosing myself, prioritizing myself when I can, elevating my own importance, and treating myself with kindness and respect. Choosing things, people, and circumstances that are beneficial to me, feel right, and serve me is another aspect of self-love.
Self-love is a constant, deliberate decision!
When I started to practice actively selecting myself over others, over hurtful situations, over unfulfilling friendships and relationships, things changed radically.

Here are a few instances from my own life that demonstrate the necessity of practicing self-love.

1. You'll begin to feel like you have greater control over your life.
I came to see that I always had options. I might make poor decisions because of guilt, shame, or fear, or I could make decisions that were empowered, in line with who I was and what felt real to me. I thus stopped attempting to satisfy others, giving

attention to men who weren't deserving of it, and engaging in activities that didn't make me feel good or satisfied.

When you begin to value yourself more, you will also come to understand that you have the power to respect your needs and wants.

2. You'll establish more rigid restrictions on romantic relationships.
Honoring my needs allowed me to become more self-assured and aggressive. I got more deliberate about dating. I stopped wasting time on bad boys and began making more informed love decisions. The end result: After years of dating failure, I finally met the love of my life.

You'll feel more empowered when you set stronger boundaries out of a place of self-love and you'll stop selecting partners who aren't right for you all the time.

3. You'll give up looking for acceptance.
The most empowering thing was this. I stopped caring about how much other people liked or approved of me as I learned to love and respect myself more. I gave up trying to win people over. This made space for me to be more sincere, less defensive, and more my genuine self.

You begin to care less about other people's opinions of you and begin living a life that is consistent with your own values when you have gained your own approval and acceptance.

4. You'll begin to make more brave and thoughtful choices.
For the sake of my own self-respect, I quit my taxing corporate career.

After fifteen years, I left London in search of a slower, more tranquil way of life.

I experienced a new love. (Doing this takes a lot of bravery if you've been hurt repeatedly!)
I became pregnant and gave birth naturally. I had previously advertised everywhere that if I ever became pregnant, I would be the first to request an epidural, so I had no idea how this had come about. Nevertheless, I paid attention to my body, and getting an epidural didn't feel right.
For my son, I became a mother. Given how much I value my freedom, this is likely the bravest thing I have ever done. However, the love I have for my son makes me forget how valuable my previous freedom was to me.

Self-love will give you the strength to get rid of things that don’t serve you and make space for things that will help you grow. Making choices that honor rather than degrade oneself is a sign that you actually love yourself.

5. You'll begin to enjoy spending time alone yourself.
To stop feeling lonely, I stopped cramming my days full with appointments, dates, and activities. I put an end to escaping into the arms of inappropriate men. I quit going out with friends just to be alone.

As a substitute, I began to do more of the activities I like, such as swimming, yoga, writing, watching movies, and meditating. Spending time alone didn't seem frightening after I had a profound connection with myself. I gave up worrying about being alone.

You'll discover that when you start liking yourself more, you'll start to feel more at ease in your own gorgeous company.

6. Your bond with yourself will get stronger.
I developed a stronger bond with myself as I spent more time alone. I started having more fun on my own, which made me less desperate for a romantic connection. I became my own friend. As I began to connect with my own inner self, I began to feel more safe as a person. I began to have greater confidence in myself. I gained more self-confidence.

Self-love helps you connect with yourself more deeply, and it also helps you connect with others more deeply. Your relationships with others strengthen as your relationship with yourself does.

7. You'll give up looking for satisfaction in partnerships.
I came to understand that I could be happy without a man by learning to love myself. I already had all the affection I needed to be content. I stopped handing my authority over to guys and started taking more responsibility for my own pleasure.

I realized that happiness permeated every aspect of my life. It wasn't in the distant future. I simply needed to shift my attention away from what I lacked and start appreciating what I did have. You'll probably feel less desperate for a romantic connection as you begin to appreciate yourself more and feel better. You'll understand that a mate is not necessary for happiness. All you have to do is smile, and the proper person will come along when they should.
How can you then begin to love yourself more? Start making everyday decisions for yourself and acting accordingly.
Make it a habit to check in with yourself each time you have to make a choice or decision.
You start by asking yourself: In this circumstance, what would feel loving?
Once you know the solution, pose these three crucial queries to yourself:
Does it feel right or nice to me?
Can it help me?

Will it give me a boost of energy?
These queries will support you in remaining honest and kind to yourself while respecting your needs and those of others.
I have a lot more I would like to say on this, but I'll save it for another article.
Let me just say that practicing self-love will change your life.

CHAPTER TWO

THE PATH TO SELF ACCEPTANCE

Self-acceptance gives you power. You can be limited in every aspect of your life if you don't accept who you are. You may not be able to realize your full potential since it undermines your confidence. High self-acceptance individuals are more tolerant of criticism. They are aware that it's acceptable to accept oneself while striving for ongoing progress. But what exactly is self-acceptance? And why are some individuals more tolerant of themselves than others? What can you do to cultivate more of it and how can it benefit you?

What does self-acceptance mean?

Accepting oneself and all of your personality qualities precisely as they are is the act of practicing self-acceptance. Whether they are good or bad, you have to accept them. Your physical and mental characteristics are included in this. Self-acceptance entails realizing that your worth extends beyond your own traits and deeds. Sometimes people refer to this as radical self-acceptance. Your self-confidence will increase and your susceptibility to criticism will decrease as a result of self-acceptance. It refers to a profound and complete acceptance of every facet of who you are, without reservation or exception. You must learn to accept the aspects of yourself that you find unfavorable or unattractive if you want to develop self-acceptance. It's crucial to recognize and appreciate your accomplishments and favorable traits. You are reminded of your strengths by reviewing your objectives and how you're doing with them. This explains why so many of us have difficulty accepting ourselves. The aspects of ourselves that we deem unacceptable are often hidden, neglected, and rejected. Instead of accepting things, here are five examples:

1. Self-acceptance aids in emotional management.

A lack of self-acceptance might have an impact on the region of your brain that controls your emotions. As a result of increased worry, tension, or rage, this might cause mental imbalance and emotional outbursts.

A lack of self-acceptance inhibits your ability to be happy. It also has an impact on your psychological and emotional health. It keeps you focused on the worst qualities of yourself, and bad emotions result from these negative ideas.

High levels of self-acceptance, on the other hand, are associated with more pleasant feelings and more psychological well-being. Self-acceptance may lift your spirits and protect you from the negative consequences of stress and sadness.

2. Self-acceptance aids in self-forgiveness.

Learning to accept oneself allows you to be less judgmental of yourself. It assists you in developing a more positive, caring, and balanced self-image

Acceptance and forgiveness, according to Dr. Srini Pillay of Harvard Medical School, go hand in hand. He claims that our incapacity to accept and forgive ourselves causes us to fragment.

These two halves — the one that needs to be forgiven and the one that needs to be forgiven — are diametrically opposed. Self-acceptance can assist you in bridging the gap, allowing you to forgive yourself for your mistakes and move on.

This is critical for your health since concentrating on the past can keep you trapped in a loop of unpleasant thoughts and feelings.

3. Self-acceptance boosts self-confidence.

Self-acceptance can increase your self-esteem. It assists you in realizing that your apparent flaws do not define you or your value.

When you are self-assured, you are more inclined to act despite your anxieties. A lack of self-acceptance, on the other hand, might hold you back and prevent you from pursuing your objectives.

Self-acceptance teaches you that failure does not define you and that it is always a learning opportunity on the road to achievement.

Confidence can also provide you with more independence. It enables you to make decisions for yourself without the need for approval from others.

4. Acceptance of oneself leads to compassion for oneself.

Self-compassion, according to self-compassion researcher Kristin Neff, is more essential for our mental and emotional well-being than self-esteem.

She defines self-compassion as treating oneself with "the same warmth and care that one would offer to a good friend." And everyone who suffers with self-acceptance would agree that we are our own worst enemies.

Self-compassion training can help you be nicer to yourself when you fail and make you more resilient to setbacks.

5. Being self-accepting allows you to be yourself.

When you don't accept yourself, you're always attempting to hide, suppress, or repress your own nature. This might leave you exhausted.

Self-acceptance allows you to present yourself more truthfully without worrying about what others think of you. When you accept yourself, you feel free to be your entire self.

What motivates acceptance of oneself?

Some people are more self-accepting by nature than others. Have you ever pondered why this is the case? Because our childhood experiences influence our mature levels of self-acceptance.

Our parents or caretakers are the first to educate us which characteristics of ourselves are acceptable and which are not.

We learn as children to accept just those aspects of ourselves that others find acceptable. We condemn the other aspects of ourselves and reject, deny, and strive to conceal them.

The difficulty is that these decisions are arbitrary. They are determined by your parents' or caregivers' values and priorities.

Different emotions, for example, are appropriate in different households. If you were up in a home where anger was frowned upon, you may find it difficult to embrace the parts of yourself that experience wrath or fury.

Your sense of self-acceptance is also affected by your parenting style. Children believe every criticism directed at them by their parents as fact.

So, if your parents were very critical or demanding, your inner critic's voice will most likely be powerful, and you may also be afraid of failure. Those who have more sympathetic parents, on the other hand, tend to be more compassionate toward themselves.

Children are also unable to differentiate between their actions and themselves. They believe that since their behavior is bad, they must also be unacceptable.

As a result, children raised by critical parents are more prone to struggle with self-acceptance. People with more positive and supportive parents are more likely to have higher levels of self-acceptance.

Self-acceptance quotes

So now you understand why self-acceptance is essential. Don't just take our word for it, though. We've compiled a list of some of our favorite thought leaders' most encouraging self-acceptance quotations.

Save them somewhere and refer to them whenever you need some motivation on your road to self-acceptance.

"Because genuine belonging occurs only when we offer our authentic, flawed selves to the world, our experience of belonging will never be larger than our level of self-acceptance." Brené Brown is a researcher.

"You can search the entire universe for someone who is more deserving of your love and devotion than you are, and that person will not be discovered." You, more than anybody else in the universe, deserve your love and affection." Sharon Salzberg is a novelist.

"Because one believes in oneself, one does not attempt to persuade others." Because one is pleased with oneself, one does not require the approval of others. Because one embraces himself or herself, the entire universe accepts him or her." Philosopher Lao Tzu

"I'm not sure I can keep like myself even today." But it was many years ago that I learnt to forgive myself. Every human being must forgive himself or herself because if you live, you will make errors – it is unavoidable. But after you've done so and recognized the error, you forgive yourself and say, 'Well, if I'd known better, I'd have done better,' and that's all." — Maya Angelou, activist and poet

"Often, it's not about becoming a new person, but about becoming the person you were born to be, but don't know how to be." Author Heath L. Buckmaster

"You are looking at a gorgeous, stunning, amazing picture!" It's elaborate and detailed, a work of commitment and love! The hues are unique; they swim and leap, trickle and adorn! And yet you chose to focus your attention on the little fly that has landed on it! "Why do you do anything like this?"

Self-esteem vs. self-acceptance

Although the two names are frequently used interchangeably, they should not be confused.

Self-esteem is derived through comparing our strengths to those of others in many facets of our lives. These are some examples:

- Health and happiness

- ? Money
- ? Beauty
- ? Strength
- ? Success
- talents and skills
- Beliefs and ethics

Our perceived value and self-worth are the foundations of our self-esteem. As a result, it pushes us to ignore or misinterpret our bad characteristics, according to Neff.

She claims that putting too much focus on self-esteem might lead to selfish, poisonous, or narcissistic conduct in order to feel better.

Self-esteem is also shaky since it is influenced by our actions and accomplishments. Relying only on one's self-esteem might make it difficult to accept defeat.

Self-acceptance is a more sophisticated and all-encompassing concept than self-esteem. It embraces all aspects of ourselves and lets us to perceive ourselves for who we truly are, independent of our exterior accomplishments.

Low self-esteem, on the other hand, might be harmful. Cultivating self-acceptance will assist you in developing more accurate and long-lasting self-esteem to healthy levels. Knowing and accepting all aspects of oneself might assist you to avoid judging and criticizing yourself.

Self-esteem fluctuates based on environmental situations. However, self-acceptance is long-lasting since it is independent of what happens in your life.

Even when things go wrong, self-acceptance may help you develop self-compassion. It can assist you in maintaining a balanced and impartial picture of oneself.

The benefit of self-compassion, according to Neff, is that you don't have to feel better than others to feel good about yourself. This differs from self-esteem, which is based on comparison.

So, when things are going well, self-esteem might offer you a temporary lift. Self-acceptance and compassion, on the other hand, will relieve you of the impulse to compare yourself to others.

Self-acceptance will provide you with satisfaction and contentment that is unrelated to external forces.

How comfortable am I with myself?

You probably already know if you have a high or low level of self-acceptance. However, to gain an idea, consider your youth.

Were your parents or primary caretakers critical and negative? Did they criticize you as a person rather than your behavior?

If you replied yes to any of these questions, you probably have a low level of self-acceptance.

The following are some indicators that you may be deficient in self-acceptance:

- You have difficulties admitting and discussing your shortcomings, flaws, and bad characteristics.
- You lack self-esteem and have a strong desire to be someone other than yourself.
- You have a pessimistic attitude on life for no apparent reason.
- You have a tendency to be self-critical and unsure about your own identity.
- If you consistently exhibit one or more of these symptoms, you most certainly have poor self-acceptance.

Meditation and other mindfulness techniques can help you gradually improve your self-acceptance. As a result, your mental and emotional well-being will improve.

Let's look at five activities you may perform every day to improve your self-acceptance.

5 activities for self-acceptance

True self-acceptance does not occur overnight. Over time, daily practice and self-care can help you steadily develop your degree of self-acceptance.

These self-acceptance activities will show you how to practice self-acceptance and love on a daily basis

1. Show gratitude

Write down three to five things you're grateful for every day. This may appear difficult at first, especially if you have a mental tendency of focusing on the bad.

However, practicing thankfulness on a daily basis might help you retrain your brain to focus on the good.

Look for the bright side of any apparently bad circumstance. Be thankful for the lessons you learnt if you failed at anything. Look for something to feel grateful about in your apparent defects as well.

2. Reframe your negative beliefs

Negative beliefs are the inner critic's voice. They inflict a great deal of pain and impede you from achieving complete self-acceptance.

Write down your negative self-perceptions and reframe them. Write it down, for example, if you feel you are a horrible person because of anything you did in the past.

After you've made your list, go over each belief and reframe it. Begin by questioning each assertion, asking yourself, "Is this true?"

Then, for each statement, replace it with more positive self-talk. "I am a decent person, but I am just human, and I occasionally make errors," for example.

3. Select your support system

Make a list of the persons with whom you spend the most time. Consider how they speak to you: are they generally positive or negative?

Identify individuals who are generally negative and consider whether it is possible to spend less time with them. You might even be able to fully remove them from your life.

This is not always practicable, such as when a close family member is involved. However, try to avoid as many negative individuals as possible. Surround yourself with individuals who respect and support you.

4. Practice meditation

A regular meditation practice can assist you in detaching from negative self-talk. This might lift your spirits and lead to more pleasant sentiments.

Meditation's purpose is to become aware of such ideas, to observe them without associating with them.

Meditation and other mindfulness activities improve psychological well-being and create inner calm. This assists you in reducing self-criticism and improving your self-image.

5. Pardon yourself

Forgiveness for mistakes and regrets in the past is a necessary step toward self-acceptance.

To transcend previous errors, do this self-forgiveness practice. It will remind you that you are only human and that you tried your best. This will assist you in letting go of regret and moving on.

Consider a scenario, deed, or blunder for which you wish to be forgiven. Write down whatever judgements you have about yourself in relation to that scenario.

For instance, you may write, "I should not have done X." "I'm such a moron."

Then, forgive yourself for holding that notion. "I forgive myself for thinking I'm foolish for that," write down. "The truth is..." and then fill in the blanks

Consider what a kind friend could say to you. "I was anxious because..." or "I was suffering and made a horrible decision," for example.

Allow yourself to be empowered by radical self-acceptance.

Accepting yourself is stepping into your power. When you establish self-acceptance, you no longer need to seek affirmation from others. Learning to accept oneself is a necessary step in taking care of your mental health.

You gain confidence in yourself and learn to accept both your talents and faults.

How to Accept Yourself: 8 Steps

It can be challenging to learn to accept every aspect of who you are, but with practice, you can master the art of self-acceptance. We can constantly work on being better versions of ourselves, but ultimately, we are who we are.

Who doesn't, after all, have strengths they are proud of and weaknesses they would rather not have? And success and failure come to each of us at different points in our lives.

Your life may become more peaceful and tranquil if you can learn to accept who you are.

How to be kind to oneself

Accept your faults.

Develop compassion for yourself.

Utilize mindfulness and present-moment awareness.

Recognize and appreciate your skills.

Set aside your inner critic.

Make contact with loved ones who value you

Get over disappointments.

Become more aware of your limitations

Self-acceptance is different from self-esteem.

Having self-esteem means feeling good about yourself and your abilities. A person with a high sense of self-worth might think they deserve good things and good experiences and that they can handle tough situations. In a 2017 study Trusted Source that looked at data from 201 teenagers, researchers found that a person's self-esteem was linked to having less anxiety, sadness, and attention problems.

Self-acceptance and self-esteem are related, but self-acceptance is the act of accepting all of who you are, including your strengths and weaknesses.

Think of it this way: self-acceptance is how you drive on that tank of gas, and self-esteem is the type of gas you use.

Why is it so hard to accept yourself as you are?

From the time we are born, our parents and other people who care for us have a big impact on how we fit into the world.

So, they have a lot of power over how we see and understand ourselves. If your caregiver supported, loved, and accepted you, your level of self-acceptance will often be very different from that of a child who had the opposite experience.

When we first start school, what matters is how we do on tests, in class, and how we fit in with our peers. All of this can help people accept themselves and feel good about themselves.

Relationships, life circumstances, and how other people treat us can all affect how easy it is for us to accept ourselves as we get older.

Many of us may find it hard to accept who we are if

Diversity, fairness, and inclusion are bad no matter where you live.

Your life has changed because you feel like a fake.

You did things that hurt others, and it cost you.

Trauma has made it hard for you to accept your past or present.

There are ways to work on accepting yourself right now, right where you are, no matter how far you have come in the past.

How to begin embracing and loving oneself

There are many ways to practice self-acceptance:

Try forgiving yourself.

Forgiving yourself can be challenging if you've ever done something to hurt someone else or act in a way, you're not proud of. However, doing so does not imply that you approve of your actions. Instead, it indicates that you are giving yourself permission to go on, accepting responsibility for what you did.

One strategy therapist employs to assist clients in developing self-forgiveness includes:

responsibility
remorse
restoration
renewal

Develop compassion for yourself.
Self-compassion entails being kind and understanding to yourself when things are hard or when you feel unworthy.

Self-compassion can be practiced in the following ways:
conversing with oneself as you would a friend.
Putting in writing any self-help suggestions.
Putting your position into perspective.
practicing self-care practices including yoga, meditation, and good diet.

Pay attention to being aware

Even though we don't always have control over what happens in life, we can try to live more on purpose every day when we wake up. You could, for example, set a goal for the following day each night. You can find your way by setting an alarm for a certain time and going for a walk before work. If you want to reach a bigger goal, like getting your dream job, try adding job hunting or updating your CV to your day.

Gratify your skills

Perhaps your friends seek you out for a sympathetic ear or because you make a mean apple pie. Or perhaps you're diligent and have a green thumb.

You can use writing down your strengths, no matter how small or significant, as a method to honor yourself.

Anytime it takes you a bit to recognize the good things about who you are, you can read the list aloud.

Put your inner critic away.

It's simple to listen to your negative ideas and be your own toughest critic.

When you sense self-criticism beginning, you can try to stop it. Then, step back and think about what you would say to a friend who was experiencing that kind of self-criticism.

Create an inner circle.

Having family and friends you can confide in and share your most intimate thoughts, anxieties, and amusing anecdotes with is the best thing in the world. Being around by people who accept you for who you are is a great way to feel welcome.

Another place to find people who share your interests is through online discussion boards or support groups

Let go of unmet expectations and enter a state of sorrow.

When your hopes and desires aren't fulfilled, it's easy to become unhappy. However, allowing yourself to feel let down is beneficial. Leaving when you're prepared may also be advantageous.

You might try remembering the effort you made to achieve that long-held goal and mentally closing that chapter in favor of a new one.

Recognize that accepting is not settling.

When you own your flaws and failures, it doesn't mean you're settling for less. In reality, being aware of your limitations can benefit your mental health in numerous ways.

Instead of focusing on how impatient you are with children, consider how well you connect with older people by routinely visiting your grandparents or volunteering at a nursing home.

A Manual for Self-Acceptance on How to Fully Accept Yourself

Many of us struggle with complete self-acceptance.

We may easily appreciate our talents, but when it comes to our failings and weaknesses, we experience a strong sensation of rejection and condemnation.

You may lack self-acceptance if you've ever been unnecessarily harsh on yourself or find it difficult to move past your mistakes or inadequacies.

Self-acceptance, sometimes referred to as self-approval, is an essential element for maintaining your psychological health; without it, it is simple to become excessively self-critical and fixate on your flaws.

These unfavorable feelings prevent you from achieving self-actualization—becoming everything you are capable of becoming—and living the life you desire.

Self-acceptance can be developed using a variety of techniques and instruments; in this article, we define self-acceptance and self-approval and present some tested methods for doing so.

You'll discover:

- Defining self-acceptance
- What distinguishes self-acceptance from self-esteem?
- What impact does self-acceptance have on your life, and why is it so crucial?
- How can you tell if you don't accept yourself as you are?
- Techniques for enhancing self-acceptance

Self-acceptance: What Is It?

The definition of self-acceptance is, as its name implies, the entire acceptance of oneself, including all of your positive and negative features.

It is much simpler to recognize our positive qualities, but in order to truly love oneself, you must also be able to accept the less attractive, less positive aspects of yourself.

It's a common misperception that self-acceptance entails giving up on oneself. that you simply quit trying to fix your flaws and inadequacies and accept yourself as you are.

Of course, that's just plain false.

True self-acceptance, on the other hand, entails being conscious of both your positive and negative characteristics without attaching any negative feelings or passing judgment on who you are.

It entails having the ability to be frank about your assets and liabilities while maintaining your sense of worth.

Simply said, accepting that your value is independent of your behaviors and character traits is the self-acceptance definition. Despite having made mistakes and having shortcomings, you are not defined by these things.

Understandably, this might be challenging, but the only way to start addressing your shortcomings and making genuine improvement is by admitting that you have them.

Self-acceptance vs self-esteem

What distinguishes self-acceptance from self-esteem, you may be asking.

Since self-acceptance and self-esteem are linked ideas, it is simple to mix them up. They are not the same thing, even though they are both essential to your psychological health.

Your perception of your own worth in comparison to others is a measure of your self-esteem. These are the benefits you provide to the world and how well you believe you stack up against the competition.

Self-esteem typically depends on outside "markers" like your achievements or accolades. At work, getting promoted can significantly boost your self-esteem, whereas getting a performance review can significantly lower it.

Clinical psychologists use the term "healthy self-esteem" to describe having a realistic, favorable view of oneself. You are confident in your worth and are aware of your advantages over others.

When the needle lies at either extreme of the spectrum, that is, when you place too much value in yourself or feel as though you are unimportant and unworthy, that is when you have unhealthy self-esteem.

Self-acceptance, on the other hand, goes considerably further than self-esteem. Acceptance that is unconditional doesn't depend on your exterior circumstances, success, or accomplishments. It involves having the capacity to accept both your excellent and poor qualities.

Self-acceptance, in contrast to self-esteem, is unconditional. You would still be able to love and be compassionate toward yourself even if you had just lost your job, your spouse, or all of your money.

Naturally, good self-esteem would be much easier to achieve for someone who has healthy self-acceptance. You can recognize your worth regardless of what is happening in your life because you rely less on outside validation.

Naturally, it would be much easier for a person with healthy self-acceptance to develop healthy self-esteem. Since you rely less on external validation, you can appreciate your value regardless of what goes on in your life.

What is the Importance of Self-Acceptance? How Does it Affect Your Life?

One of the six aspects in the six-factor model of psychological well-being, unconditional self-acceptance is crucial for your mental and emotional well.

High levels of self-acceptance are associated with improved mood control, less depressive symptoms, and an increase in pleasant feelings.

Your psychological health suffers without self-acceptance, which hinders your efforts to build a happier, more successful life for yourself.

For instance, those who have a negative body image may reject their bodies because they don't accept themselves. They feel unsightly and inferior to others, thinking that their physique is a failure.

They experience body-related shame, self-consciousness, unease, and anxiety as a result of this perspective. They then get obsessed with their physical appearance, weight, food, and calories, which may ultimately end in an eating problem.

High self-acceptance individuals are aware that their physical appearance does not define them.

They can accept that starving and crash diets are simply other forms of self-abuse and learn to love both their interior and external selves.

Self-compassion increases when self-acceptance is high. They are able to make healthy, positive changes to reach their optimal body weight because they are capable of loving and respecting themselves.

Following self-acceptance, you also benefit psychologically in various ways, including:

- Greater freedom to be who you are
- The capacity to take chances without being concerned about the results
- Less concern about failing
- Living for yourself will help you be more genuine (and not for others)
- A greater sense of worth
- When you fail, be more compassionate and less critical of yourself.
- Greater autonomy and independence over your own life
- Less despite trying to gain others' praise
- A rise in self-esteem

- **What Signs Point to Low Self-Acceptance?**
- Many people struggle with low self-esteem, and for good reason—research demonstrates that before the age of eight, our ability to accept ourselves completely depends on our caregivers.
- If you grew up hearing from your parents that you weren't good enough, smart enough, attractive enough, etc., you may have developed the idea that you were only acceptable under certain circumstances. Your level of self-acceptance would have probably been negatively impacted by this.
- Currently, if you exhibit any of the following signs, you may struggle with self-acceptance:
- You frequently adopt a pessimistic outlook.
- It can be challenging to admit your flaws or mistakes.
- You constantly doubt your identity or are critical of yourself all the time.
- You wished you were someone other than who you are now.

- We all experience these symptoms occasionally, but if you notice that you consistently display these behavioral patterns, it would be wise to improve your self-acceptance.

How Can You Come to Accept Yourself?

You could now be wondering, "What is the secret to self-acceptance? How can I accomplish it on my own? It might be difficult to achieve unconditional self-acceptance, especially when it calls for overcoming years of subconscious training.

But with time and practice, you may improve your self-acceptance by using the tips and techniques listed below.

Step 1 Begin with forgiving yourself.

Self-compassion is the first step in learning to accept oneself.

Move on after realizing that you did the best you could at the time and that you can no longer undo your past mistakes and shortcomings.

Exercise in Self-Acceptance: Visualize your prior self as a different individual. Remind yourself that you can only change the aspects of your present self that you are now in control of.

This type of mental restructuring leads to self-compassion. You start to see that what you despise about yourself right now is a result of judging your former self in light of your present self, who was the one who needed to make that error in the first place.

Many of us, according to Marisa Peer, bestselling author and creator of Rapid Transformational Therapy® (RTT®), are our own harshest critics, and this critical mindset keeps us from learning self-compassion.

But you can start to forgive yourself and build a better relationship with yourself by altering the way you talk to yourself.

The essential first step in achieving self-acceptance is having this mindset. Accept responsibility for your past errors and shortcomings, but try not to berate yourself. You did the best you could at the time, so be kind to yourself.

Step 2: Engage in mindfulness.

Since a lot of the self-talk, we have is subconscious, we often don't even realize when we are rejecting ourselves.

failures, but do not beat yourself up about it. Forgive yourself—after all, you did the best you could at the time.

Spend some time observing your thoughts and emotions. Do you get anxiety when you consider a certain aspect of your life? What flaws in yourself do you find embarrassing? Which aspects do you make an effort to not consider?

These are challenging questions, but the answers will help you realize which aspects of yourself you have the hardest time accepting.

Self-Acceptance Exercise: It could be useful to record your feelings during the day in a journal and put these down as a self-acceptance exercise. This will help you identify any dysfunctional habits or thought patterns that prevent you from accepting yourself.

Do not forget to engage in self-compassion exercises while performing this one. Remember that the purpose of this exercise is just to raise your consciousness of the aspects of yourself that you have been unconsciously rejecting, not to judge you.

Step 3: Accept your emotions, both positive and negative.

It makes sense that exploring aspects of yourself that you find challenging may elicit strong negative emotions.

Your subconscious's first reaction whenever you had these emotions in the past was to push them aside. Your mind functions in a manner similar to how our nervous systems deliberately avoid physical pain by actively avoiding mental and emotional anguish.

The issue is that your subconscious is only putting off dealing with it, which is a temporary fix. You must face these emotions head-on if you want to accept yourself.

Although your first inclination would be to try to ignore these negative feelings, resist doing so this time.

Self-acceptance Exercise: Investigate that emotion with curiosity and aloofness. Imagine that you are your best friend; how would you treat them if they arrived hurt?

After allowing yourself to experience these unfavorable feelings for a bit, consider what you can take away from it. What constructive way can you think of to make this feeling?

During this activity, you might also feel good; if you do, you might automatically reject them; try not to. Accept these wonderful feelings, be proud of who you are, and remember that both the good and negative things in your life were earned.

Step 4: Let go of perfection

One of the biggest barriers to unconditional self-acceptance is the belief that you must be perfect.

We unavoidably make mistakes and acquire defects as humans. Low self-acceptance individuals could try to hide these defects or stay away from challenging situations.

Because their potential isn't being fully realized due to their failure-related fear, they wind up leading inauthentic lives.

You'll be more able to accept yourself if you realize that your flaws make you special and that failing is a part of life.

Don't define yourself by your successes or failures to aid you in this activity. Instead, recognize that you are the most valuable person to yourself, despite of the errors and failings you have made. This is to say, grasp that your value is inherent in who you are.

Being honest and accepting of yourself, flaws and all, becomes much simpler when you let go of the pressure to be flawless.

Step 5: Abandon self-comparison

Because we continuously compare ourselves to others, it might be difficult to build self-acceptance. There is a sudden pressure for people to look flawless on their social media feed, especially with the introduction of social media.

By giving you the impression that everyone you know or follow leads a joyful, ideal life, this prevents you from appreciating your own.

According to studies, persons who use social media are more inclined to objectify themselves and compare themselves to others. In general, people with social media profiles had worse mental health, more body shame, and lower self-esteem.

Keep in mind that genuine self-acceptance is unconditional; it is not based on how successful you think you are in comparison to your peers. Because your life is completely individual to you, you will always value it.

When you stop comparing yourself to other people, you start to go within and concentrate on yourself. As your need for external approval decreases, you begin turning to yourself for approval, which is a step toward self-acceptance.

Step 6: Actively participate in your own development

It might be a challenging task to learn to accept yourself. It is not something that should be hurried and it won't happen overnight. It is something that will require a lot of effort, focus, and patience.

We are aware that if you are working on your self-acceptance on your own, it may be difficult to achieve.

Self-acceptance and confidence are inextricably linked. You must possess the self-assurance necessary to accept yourself as you are, to navigate the world in your true self, and to

remain as you are once you have gained the behavior

THE IMPORTANCE OF SELF-LOVE AND SELF-ACCEPTANCE

The Value of Loving and Accepting Yourself

"When we start accepting who we are, progress occurs." Juan Vanier

Because society expects us to a level of perfection, we frequently adopt standards for ourselves that are unreasonably high. We frequently fail to recognize that even people we hold up as being perfect have flaws.

The ability to love and accept oneself is crucial for both health and pleasure. These traits have a real, discernible impact on our emotional, mental, and physical health. When we reject who we are, we cut ourselves off from the force that sustains life. This process eventually erodes our connection to the life energy. And this has negative health effects.

When we don't accept who we are, we are effectively wearing ourselves down from the inside out. And when we fight ourselves, guess who loses? It's important to recognize that we all have flaws. Sometimes everyone makes mistakes. You shouldn't try to avoid making mistakes at all costs. Through it, one of the best ways to grow is possible.

Accepting our positive and bad features and resolving internal disputes are essential to our health and happiness. You also can't do much in the outside world if you don't deal with your inner world.

ways to tell if you don't love yourself

putting your happiness in other people's hands. If they don't love themselves, no one can be happy with themselves. They will try to micromanage and control others in an effort to feel better about themselves. In essence, they are energy vampires.

having to defend yourself continuously. People who struggle with self-acceptance tend to exaggerate their strengths and boast in order to win over others. They work to persuade everyone who is listening to believe what they are saying, even when they privately don't. Never forget that true love never boasts. Anyone who is boastful is a person who has self-doubt.

They are unable to decide because they require other people's approval or want their opinions. In essence, they seek the respect and focus of others.

They are perplexed as to why they keep having terrible luck so frequently. They complain and blame others for their difficulties while disregarding the fact that how they feel about themselves affects what happens to them.

They have a self-centered worldview, therefore they are preoccupied with their own problems all the time. They frequently have a negative view of themselves because they think everyone is talking about them.

They keep going back to the people or circumstances that make them angry or hurt because they want to prove their worth, even if they know in their hearts that it is impossible.

indicators of problems with self-acceptance

A number of issues with one's physical, mental, and emotional health are brought on by harsh self-judgment and criticism. In order to resolve these issues as soon as possible, it's imperative to be aware of the warning indications that you don't accept and love yourself.

As a result of rejecting who you are, low self-esteem results. People who force themselves to think and act like someone else feel as though they are living a lie because it's not a life they built. Another component of denying who you are is ignoring your inner voice, which constantly exhorts you to be who you are. What happened? You'll experience stress, overwhelm, and self-resentment.

becoming victimized, which involves seeking acceptance or believing what others say about you. In the end, you advance someone else's goals rather than your own.

Not believing in yourself will eventually lead to low self-confidence because you won't have faith in yourself. As soon as you start to feel sorry for yourself and despise yourself, your growth and development will be put on hold.

Inability to inspire and motivate oneself to engage in healthy activities including obtaining adequate sleep, eating a balanced diet, and exercising frequently leads to inactivity.

Self-love versus self-acceptance

Even while these two concepts are connected, they are not the same. Self-love is the value or worth you place on yourself, whereas self-acceptance is a general affirmation of who you are.

Accepting both our positive and negative sides is the secret to self-acceptance. This translates into complete acceptance of who you are. Recognizing and accepting your shortcomings or weaknesses shouldn't prevent you from accepting yourself entirely.

If you want to learn to love yourself, you must acknowledge the parts of yourself that you are not yet ready to accept. The secret to loving yourself is to accept yourself entirely. Once you stop criticizing yourself, you can only achieve this. Research indicates that when we stop being so critical of ourselves, our self-esteem rises.

What causes someone to accept who they are?

Children can only love themselves to the extent that they feel loved by the adults in their environment, much like with self-love (especially parents). According to psychologists, children are unable to acquire a sense of self that is separate from what their parents or guardians have taught them until they are eight years old.

Consequently, if a parent was unable to express the idea that you are acceptable, he or she trained you to have a cloudy perception of yourself. The supportive messages you got from your parents were mostly a result of your behavior. Unfortunately, many of your acts weren't tolerated or appreciated by them. Finally, you start to think poorly of yourself.

Parental judgment goes beyond expressing disapproval for a specific behavior pattern. For instance, our parents might tell us that we are rude, ungrateful, disagreeable, or ugly. As a result, you start highlighting your shortcomings. Then comes self-criticism gradually.

It is impossible to avoid rearing our kids in the same manner that we were. We would find a way to continue this self-deprecation if our parents assigned blame, ignored us, or physically punished us. According to Robert Holden, contentment and acceptance of oneself go hand in hand. How content and in love with yourself you are will depend on how much self-acceptance you have. As you come to accept yourself more, you'll be joyful. You will only experience happiness to the extent that you think you deserve it.

How to develop love and acceptance for oneself

Every time you feel worn out, fatigued, or detest yourself, you are turning your thoughts and feelings against yourself. Additionally, this will make life challenging for both you and your loved ones. To help you cultivate self-love and self-acceptance so you may succeed both personally and professionally, here are a few tried-and-true tips.

You should put more effort into bettering yourself than into trying to be like other people. This involves creating objectives and success metrics. Remember that liking oneself is not the same as being selfish. How can you expect others to love you if you don't? In order to promote the wellbeing of others, you must take care of your own physical and emotional wellbeing. Never be scared to focus and set priorities for yourself.

Stop trying to change who you are and start accepting yourself warts and all. You can just acknowledge that you already possess all you need to succeed and stop making such a big effort to change who you are or chase butterflies. Any alterations or adjustments will occur spontaneously, much like a flower opening. There is no reason for you to change since you are the only person in the entire world who is precisely like you. You are a unique and remarkable individual.

Face your fears We all experience horrible events. We all have burdens that prevent us from taking chances and hurting ourselves. Our fear of failing keeps us from realizing our greatest potential. Because they are afraid of the unknown, most people prefer to stay in their familiar surroundings. To avoid becoming startled when making modifications and alterations, it's imperative to move slowly. To begin, make a list of everything you have been afraid to do. It can entail talking to your crush, making connections at a key event, or requesting a raise from your boss. Face it by beginning with a little step. Find out what is making you hesitant. A big triumph is made up of many smaller ones.

As this will affect how far you can develop in both your personal and professional life, surround yourself with positive people. Being around negative people will not help you become a positive person. Your mind won't feel any better if the worst that the world has to offer happens. Therefore, it's important to choose your business carefully. Being around positive individuals will help you deal with your worries. Aside from that, focus on the positive aspects of life. Remember that your mind is like a piece of ground. If you give it enough time to grow, it will produce scrumptious fruits. If you don't cultivate it, there will be weeds growing naturally. Once they get control, it will also be very difficult to get rid of them.

Don't take offense personally – If someone or something offends you, don't take it personally. Never assume that you comprehend what they are saying. Refrain from defending and safeguarding oneself. If you stop taking things personally, you'll notice that everyone is making an effort to make things work. They can also be having a bad day without your fault.

Until you are capable of forgiving yourself and others, you cannot grow and thrive. Keep in mind that extending forgiveness is a selfish act. You show them forgiveness so that you will have the energy to focus on your own growth. Take ownership of your mistakes. Nobody is perfect. Being overly critical of yourself or others won't make you more successful.

Forget about the ideal and focus on improving yourself. Being perfect is not necessary to move on to the following level. If you remain focused on your progress, you'll succeed. There is always room for improvement, regardless of how well you perform.

Never give up; if you fall, you must get back up and keep going. Failure teaches us more about ourselves than prosperity does. Decide what has to be done and then just do it. At the end of the day, honor your bravery in pursuing your objectives.

Conclusion

You are a unique and remarkable individual. Anything you set your mind to; you can achieve. Nothing in the world can prevent you from accomplishing your goals as long as you fully accept and love yourself.

Acknowledgement

THANKS FOR READING AND I HOPE YOU TRUELY FIND HAPPINESS AND PEACE

ROXANNE HILL

www.ingramcontent.com/pod-product-compliance
Lightning Source LLC
LaVergne TN
LVHW080817170826
845678LV00011B/2040

* 9 7 9 8 3 5 2 0 3 7 2 9 4 *